The little guid
SCIENCE

Catherine de Duve

An interactive adventure in the land of discoveries

BIG BANG

15 billion years ago, the universe came into being in a huge explosion, the Big Bang. For a fraction of a second, the temperature rose to around 10 billion degrees, and then cooled almost at once.
The universe was originally a gas formed of invisible particles, which bounced around and off each other, chaotically.
Since its birth, the universe has not stopped growing. It is expanding.

- 360 MILLION YEARS
First steps on earth, as the first vertebrates emerge from the water

- 580 MILLION YEARS
First animals with shells

- 600 MILLION YEARS
First animals, jellyfish and plants, algae

- 4.5 BILLION YEARS
Birth of the Sun and the solar system. The Earth is formed.

- 3.8 BILLION YEARS
Life appears on Earth

- 3 BILLION YEARS
Bacteria and the first cells appear

- 15 BILLION YEARS
Big Bang. Elementary particles, electrons, protons, photons... atomic nuclei

- 12 BILLION YEARS
Galaxies formed

THE UNIVERSE IS BORN

- 230 MILLION YEARS
Birth of the first dinosaurs

- 65 MILLION YEARS
The dinosaurs disappear and mammals evolve

- 4 MILLION YEARS
Australopithecus, man's first ancestor

- 2.5 MILLION YEARS
Homo habilis uses the first tools

- 630 000 YEARS
Homo erectus, a hunter

- 150 000 YEARS
Homo sapiens neanderthalensis

- 40 000 YEARS
Homo sapiens sapiens, our closest ancestor

- 1 BILLION YEARS
Cells with nuclei emerge

- 2 BILLION YEARS
Oxygen formed in the atmosphere

DINOSAURS

Dinosaurs lived on earth before man existed! It was hotter then than it is now. Dinosaurs first appeared 200 million years ago, and their name means 'terrible lizard'! The dinosaurs were reptiles. They laid eggs. There are still animals living today which are descended from the dinosaurs: birds.

The dinosaurs die out

Dinosaurs died out because they couldn't adapt to change. The theory is that 65 million years ago a volcanic eruption took place, and a meteorite (a huge rock) fell to earth, causing terrible tidal waves and earthquakes.

Huge clouds of dust blocked out the sky. The light couldn't get through. Plants and trees stopped growing. The dinosaurs couldn't find any food, and the temperature fell.

These cold-blooded animals couldn't adjust their body temperature to the new climate. Other animals replaced them: mammals.

The terrible lizards disappeared for ever.

PREHISTORY

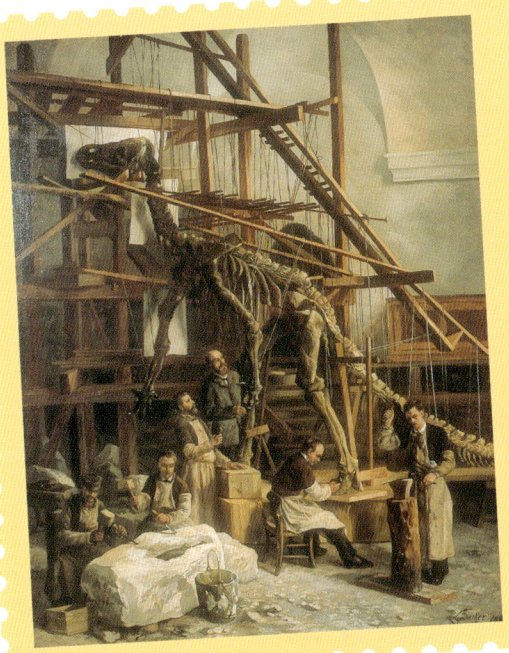

Discovery

Iguanodons were found in Belgium.
When digging in the coal mines in Bernissart, some men discovered huge fossilised skeletons.
This dinosaur was 10 metres long and 5 metres high.

INFO
The biggest dinosaur was 28 metres long. The heaviest weighed 70 tonnes.

Draw your own imaginary dinosaurs.

FOSSILS

Palaeontologists search the ground for remains.
They find bones, teeth and fossils.
Fossils are imprints left by plants or animals.
Their veins or skeletons have gradually turned into stone, over millions of years.

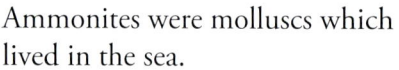

Ammonites were molluscs which lived in the sea.
They disappeared at the same time as the dinosaurs.
Fossils help us to rediscover many species which no longer exist.
They help us to reconstitute how live has evolved.

CHARLES DARWIN

Charles Darwin (1809-1882) was a British naturalist. He sailed round the world in a boat for five years. He observed and listed the various species of animals and plants. He saw that animals and plants survive if they adapt to change. Otherwise they disappear.
This is the law of natural selection.

PALAEONTOLOGY

Fossilisation of a dinosaur

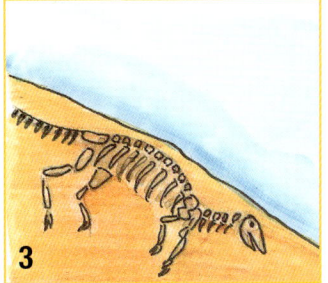

1. The dead dinosaur falls into a swamp and sinks.

2. Its body decomposes under water.

3. All that is left is the skeleton. Gradually, mud and sand cover the animal's skeleton, one layer after the next.

4. Because of their weight, these layers harden under pressure and turn into rock. The calcium in the dinosaur bones turns into stone. It becomes a fossil.

5. Wind and rain erode the rock. The dinosaur fossil may come to the surface millions of years after its death.

Whose are these fossilised eggs?
○ chicken
○ bird
○ ostrich
○ dinosaur

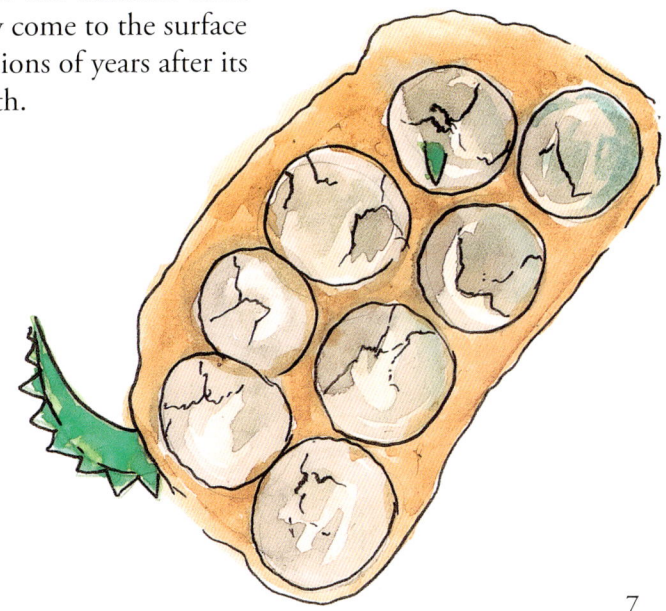

LIFE UNDER THE MICROSCOPE

Life emerges gradually... 12 billion years ago after the Big Bang! It began in the water, as little bubbles of life, cells.

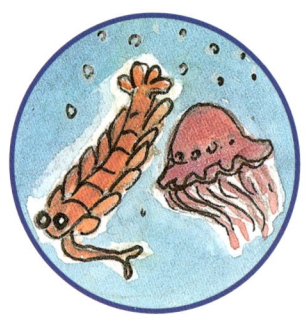

The first plants were tiny algae.
The first animals were soft like jellyfish.
The first men had a brain which developed in the course of evolution.

Who is the cleverest?
Look at these skulls, and see how man has evolved.
Put them in the right order.

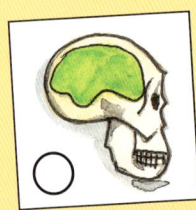 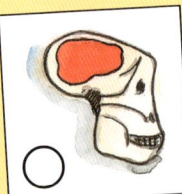 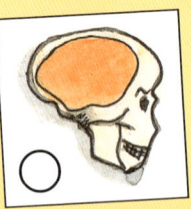 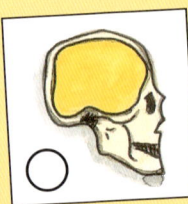 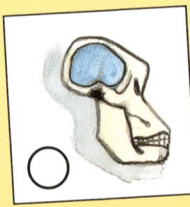

1. *Australopithecus* – the first man (4 million years ago).
2. *Homo habilis* – makes stone tools, hunts and picks fruit (2 million years ago).
3. *Homo erectus* tames fire (1.5 million years ago).
4. *Homo sapiens* neanderthalensis is the first to adapt to the cold climate. He uses fire to keep warm and wears clothes (150,000 years ago).
5. *Homo sapiens sapiens* is just like us. He uses razors, fine needles made out of bone to sew clothes out of animal skins and decorates these with feathers and shells. He is a farmer (40,000 years ago).

TIP
Maybe you've heard of one of your *Homo sapiens sapiens* ancestors? Cro-magnon man.

ANTHROPOLOGY - BIOLOGY

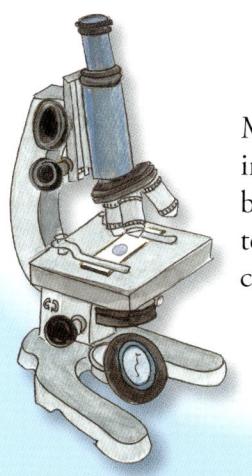

Microscopes allow us to look at infinitely tiny things. There are billions of cells in our body, invisible to the naked eye. They multiply and create life!

Let's go to the laboratory and look at a cell through a microscope.

Cytoplasm is the substance which contains all the elements surrounding the nucleus.

The **plasma membrane** protects the cell. It provides contact with the outer surface of the cell.

The **nucleus** contains the DNA molecule, a very complex chemical substance. It enables all living beings to develop, to function and to reproduce..

The **lysosomes** act as the cell's stomach. They absorb the elements in the cell which are too old or ill.

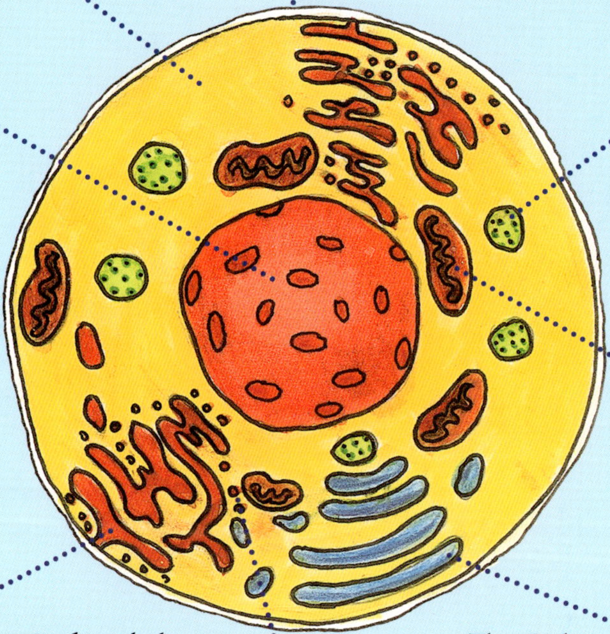

The **mitochondria** produce the cell's energy.

The **endoplasmic reticulum** helps the ribosomes to move around.

The **Golgi apparatus** stores the surplus proteins.

The **ribosomes** are little chemical balls which synthesise proteins.

HAVE YOU EVER COUNTED THE STARS?

To observe the universe, man invented an instrument which let him see better and further. In 1610, the Italian scholar Galileo made a telescope. At the ends of a lead tube, he placed one convex lens and one concave lens. Thanks to this instrument, he discovered many new stars which, up to then, had been invisible to the naked eye.

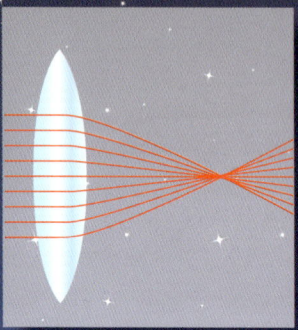

Convex lens Light rays

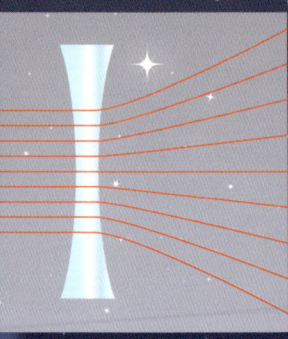

Concave lens Light rays

Let's go to the observatory

In the observatory, astronomers use a transit telescope to observe the stars passing the meridians. With a refracting telescope, you can see further than with a transit telescope, since the light is reflected by a concave mirror. The bigger the lens, the more light it collects and the further the astronomer will see.

TIP
Venus is a planet which is sometimes known as the 'Shepherd's star'. It's not a star, but a planet which shines because it reflects the light of the Sun, like the Moon.

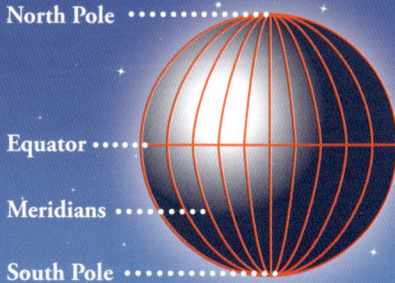

North Pole
Equator
Meridians
South Pole

ASTRONOMY

A star is a vast ball of fire, shining in the universe.

The Sun is the closest star to Earth. It is only 150 million kilometres away! It has been around for 4.6 billion years. It is half way through its life.

Before it dies, the Sun will grow and will become a giant star which will increase Earth's temperature to 2,000°C!

Nine planets turn around the Sun and form the solar system.

They are made up of gas and residues from the Sun. Planets don't shine like stars. Shooting stars are blocks of rock, iron or nickel, sometimes covered with ice, which burn as they move through the atmosphere.

Where am I? Name the planets.

- **Mercury** is the smallest planet and closest to the Sun.
- **The Earth** is known as the blue planet. Water covers more than 70% of its surface.
- **Mars** is called the red planet. Its colour comes from the dust and ferrous rocks which cover it.
- **Jupiter** is the biggest and heaviest planet.
- **Saturn** is surrounded by many satellites. Dust from the satellites forms rings around this planet.
- **Pluto** is the planet which is furthest from the Sun, and the smallest. It is dark and icy.
- **Venus** is covered in scorching-hot, volcanic desert plains. It is the planet which shines most brightly.
- **Uranus** is a blue-green colour because of the clouds of methane surrounding it.
- **Neptune** is covered in ice and liquid. It's the windiest planet. It has a great dark spot on it.

PHENAKISTOSCOPE, DECEIVER OF THE EYES

In 1832, the Belgian physicist **Joseph Plateau** invented the phenakistoscope. What a complicated name! It means deceiver of the eyes. He rotated a disk with sixteen pictures, which break down a movement into tiny changes. This was the beginning of the cinema and of animation!

The first animation

The rapid succession of images forms a mini-film which you can watch through a slit. A phenomenon known as 'retinal persistence' gives the impression of movement. This means that the previous image stays on the eye's retina until the next image comes along. As these images are slightly different, they give the illusion of movement.

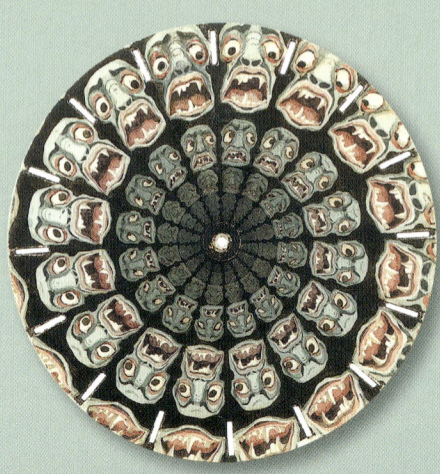

KINETICS - OPTICS

Experiment

Concentrate very hard for two minutes, fixing your eyes on a coloured square, and then look at a white ceiling. What do you see appear?

Experiment

Look at this picture while turning your open book round and round. What do you think you see?

13

PROFESSOR PICCARD'S GONDOLA

The Swiss physicist **Auguste Piccard** (1884-1962) was the first person to go up into the stratosphere. In 1931, he boarded an airtight metal gondola. He went up to a great altitude (16,201 metres)! That's very, very high. Almost twice the height of the highest mountain in the world. He also went underwater. In 1953, he went down, with his son, to a depth of 3,150 metres on board his bathyscaphe.

 Look at the photo of Auguste Piccard. He inspired the writer Hergé to create one of the characters in the Tintin books. Is his name:
◯ Professor Octopus,
◯ Professor Calculus,
◯ Professor Minibus?

Hot air balloons

Long before Piccard, in 1783, the Montgolfier brothers created the first balloon to rise into the air. On the ground, a fire heats the air inside the balloon. When the air in the balloon heats up and expands, it takes up more room and becomes lighter than the air around it. The balloon then rises.

PHYSICS

THE ATMOSPHERE is a thick layer of air surrounding Earth. It is vital for life. It protects us from the Sun's rays and gives us the oxygen we need to breathe.

AIR is a mixture of several gases: 78% nitrogen, 21% oxygen and 1% other rare gases. The air has existed for millions of years and varies depending on the climate, plants and human activities. It is constantly being recycled. We need to protect it from being polluted and destroyed.
At a high altitude, air becomes rare and loses its blue colour. Above the atmosphere there is no air. Up there, everything is silent. There is no sound in space. Sound waves can't pass through an empty space.

Draw the highest mountain in the world: Mount Everest in the Himalayas, 8,848 metres high.

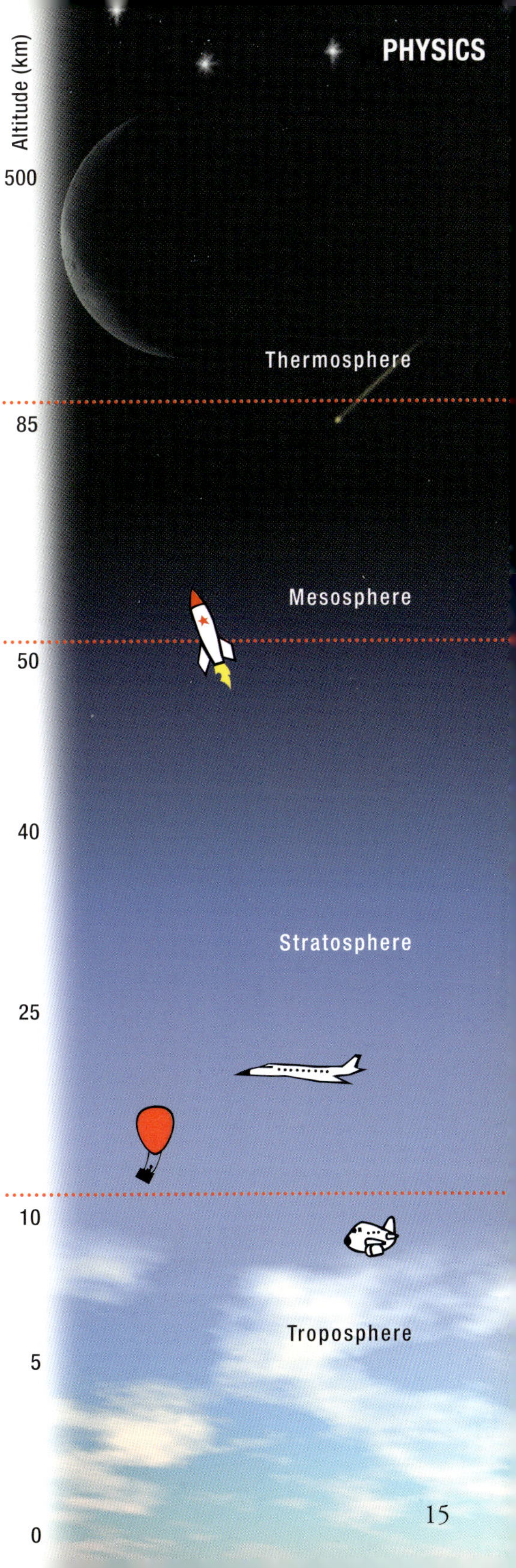

Altitude (km)

- 500 — Thermosphere
- 85
- Mesosphere
- 50
- 40 — Stratosphere
- 25
- 10
- 5 — Troposphere
- 0

ANTARCTICA

Adrien de Gerlache de Gomery (1866-1934) was a Belgian who loved adventures. For years he prepared for a major scientific expedition to the South Atlantic ocean.

He bought a boat, the Belgica, and formed a team of 19 members, sailors and scientists.

Draw the Belgica on the map and mark its return journey in colour (the dotted line on the map).

SCIENTIFIC EXPLORATION

The *Belgica* was a three-masted sailing boat, 30 metres long. Built in 1884 for seal-hunting, it was specially strengthened to protect it from ice floes. A laboratory for zoological and oceanographic research was built on deck. The *Belgica* left the port of Antwerp on 16 August 1897. Destination the South Pole! Overwintering in the frozen ocean, the team explored the white continent and listed their discoveries. Disaster! The boat was trapped in ice for many long months. Finally it broke free and returned home safely on 5 November 1899.

Circle the animal which comes from the South Pole.

ELECTRICITY

The term 'electricity' comes from the word 'electron'. Electrons are minuscule invisible particles which circle the nucleus of an atom, made up of protons and neutrons.

Atoms are in a state of equilibrium if they have the same number of electrons and protons. But electrons easily break free of atoms, and this movement creates an electric current.

Atoms are the smallest element of all matter. Your hair, air, water and your book are all made up of atoms.

 Colour the photons (p+) in red, the neutrons (n°) in green and the electrons (e-) in blue.

Static electricity

Comb your hair very quickly with a plastic comb. Can you hear a slight crackling sound? Is your hair standing on end?

Why? When your comb comes into rapid contact with the atoms in your hair, it becomes loaded with electrons. The hair atoms have lost some negatively-charged electrons, and your hair now has a positive charge. The atoms in your hair need to balance themselves out, so they are attracted to the negative charge of the electrons on the comb. When your comb again makes contact with your hair, the phenomenon comes to an end.

Experiment

Rub a balloon against a woollen jumper, then put it against a wall. It will stay there when you let go!

PHYSICS

The battery

In 1800, the Italian physicist **Alessandro Volta** (1745-1827) invented the first electric battery. He piled up discs of zinc and copper separated by cloth impregnated with diluted acid. The chemical reaction which takes place between the acid and the two metals produces a continuous electric current. The inventor saw small sparks. This was the first electric generator. The volt, the unit of measurement, was named after Volta.

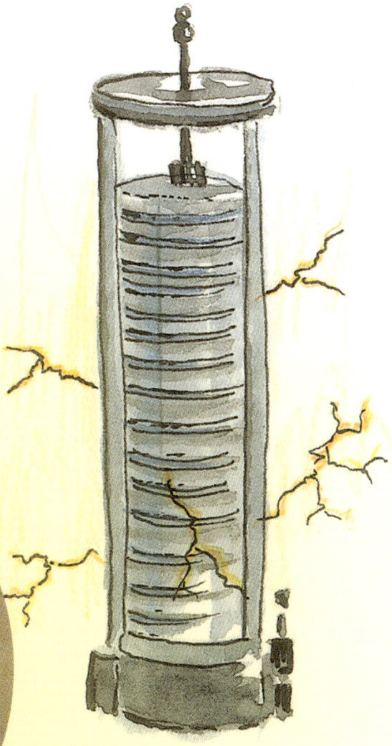

The light bulb

The American inventor **Thomas Edison** (1847-1931) developed one of the first light bulbs. An electric current is passed through an incandescent, highly heat-resistant filament, which becomes very hot. Since it is contained in a vacuum within the light bulb, it does not burn up, but shines.

ZÉNOBE GRAMME'S DYNAMO

In 1870, the Belgian **Zénobe Gramme** invented a dynamo. An electric dynamo is a machine which generates electricity by converting movement (mechanical energy) into electrical energy. It works as an electricity generator. The dynamo contains a permanent magnet and a loop of electrical wire which rotates around the magnet's two poles.

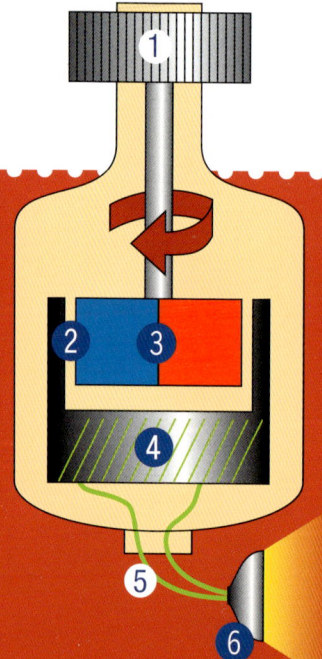

The dynamo in your bike

Look how your bike lamp works. The wheel on your bike turns a cog (1) in the magnetic field (2) of the magnet (3). The force of the field moves the electrons in the wire coil (4), which creates an electric current. The current circulating in the wire (5) lights up the bulb in the lamp (6).

MAGNETISM

Attraction

Magnets have two opposite poles at either end: the North pole and the South pole, which attract each other. They are linked by magnetic field lines. This is called an attraction field.

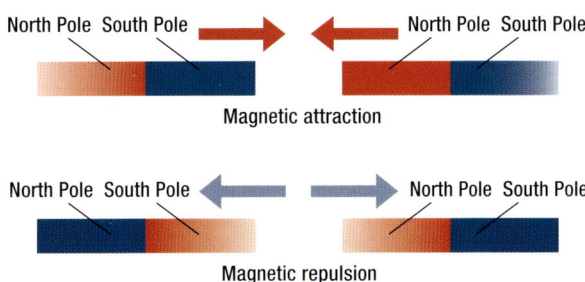

Experiment

Find a magnet. There might be one on your fridge. Place some objects near the magnet: a piece of paper, a screw, a nail, an eraser, a pencil, a paperclip, a pin, some sugar, some silver foil, some needles. Which objects are attracted to the magnet?

The biggest magnet in the world

The Earth acts as a magnet, with a magnetic field and two poles, the North pole and the South pole. This is called terrestrial magnetism. Navigators and explorers use a compass to find their way. The needle points to the North and the South.

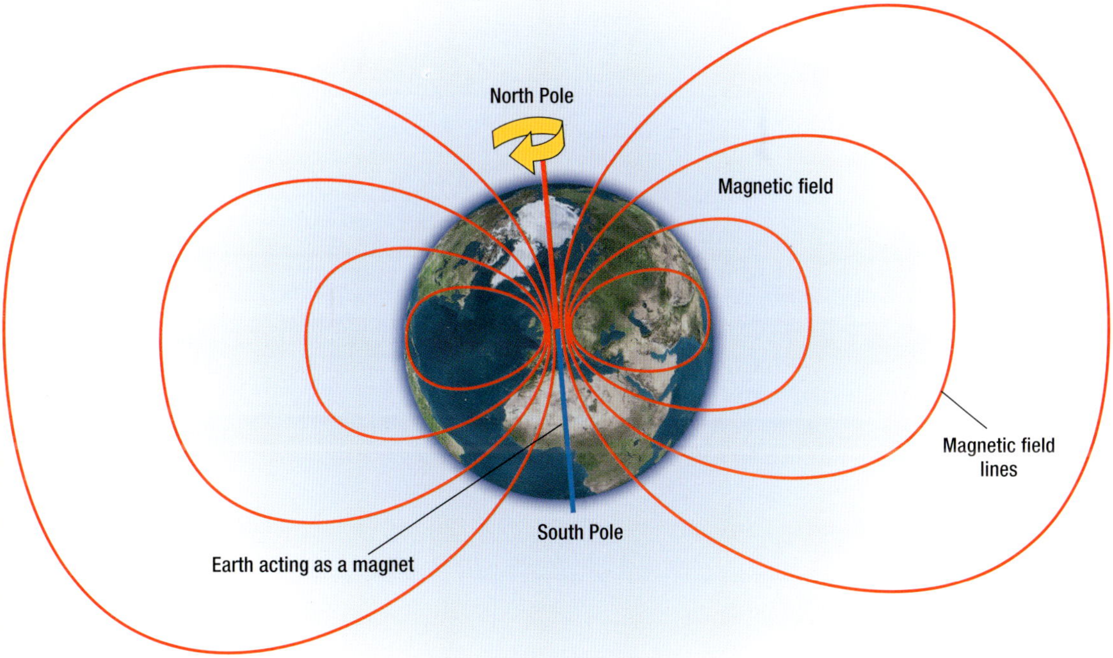

STORMS

A storm is approaching, with its big black clouds, heavy with rain. They are charged with static electricity. These are cumulonimbus clouds. Electricity is discharged from the cloud as a very powerful spark. We see this as lightning zigzagging across the sky. It seeks out the most humid zones in the air. If it touches the ground or another cloud, it returns immediately by the same path. Shortly afterwards, you hear the thunderclap.

Why do we hear the thunder after we see the lightning?

The speed of sound varies, and is on average 330 m/sec. Sound travels more slowly than light, which travels at a speed of 300,000 km/sec.

TIP
If you hear thunder 10 seconds after seeing lightning, that means that the lightning is around 3 km away. There are 2,000 storms raging on Earth at any one time.

MAGNETISM AND ELECTRICITY

Lightning is a form of electricity

The air is made up of a multitude of invisible atoms. Clouds are made up of particles of dust or of ice rubbing against each other. As they do so, the electrons break free from their atoms. A large mass of electrons collect in the base of the cloud.

The clouds are charged with static electricity. When there are too many electrons, these negatively-charged electrons are attracted to the Earth, which is positively charged. Lightning is produced, which heats up the air. The air expands. The thunder explodes. Lightning is an electrical discharge.

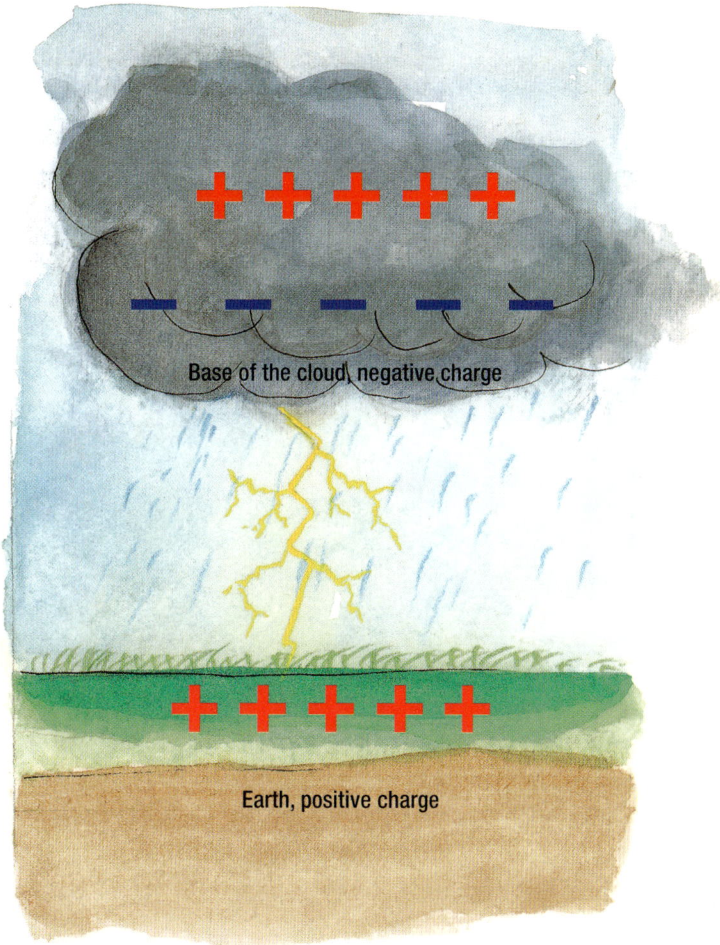

How to keep safe

- During a storm, never stand on top of a hill.
- Never take shelter under an isolated tree.
- Never stay in a swimming pool or near water.
- A car is a good place to shelter. The lightning will travel around the outside of the body of the car, without affecting it.
- The best thing is to stay at home and to unplug electrical appliances.

Base of the cloud, negative charge

Earth, positive charge

LIGHTNING CONDUCTORS

A lightning conductor is a metal rod which protects houses from lightning. You put it at the highest point on the roof. It is connected to the ground by a metal cable, so it conducts the lightning charge into the ground, where it is discharged safely.

MAGNETISM AND ELECTRICITY

The first lightning conductor

In 1752, the American **Benjamin Franklin** flew a kite during a storm. He risked his life to prove that lightning was a form of electricity. The inventor attached a metal key to the end of the wet kite-string.
Dampness attracts lightning, and metal conducts electricity. The key, linked to the ground by a cord, conducted the electricity discharged by the lightning into the ground. This is how Franklin invented the lightning conductor.

In this picture, where would you put the lightning conductor? Where would you take shelter?

THE TELEGRAPH

The first telegraph was invented in 1837 by two Englishmen, **Cooke** and **Wheatstone**. You send a message from a transmitting telegraph to a receiving telegraph by sending electrical signals. These move magnetic needles which point to letters. A sequence of letters forms a word. The system needs many bulky cables. In 1866, an underwater cable was laid to link Europe to America.

Cooke

Wheatstone

Morse code

The American painter **Samuel Morse** (1791-1872) invented an effective telegraph system, using 'Morse code'. Letters and figures are replaced by dots and dashes which are printed on a roll of paper. It's a quick and efficient method.

This message is in Morse code. Can you decipher it?

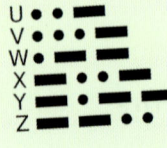

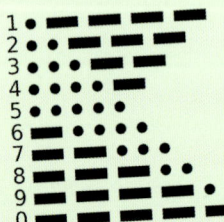

26

TELECOMMUNICATIONS

THE TELEPHONE

In America, the Scotsman **Alexander Graham Bell** and his assistant discover that you can convert a voice into an electric current! They've invented the telephone! It's 1876.

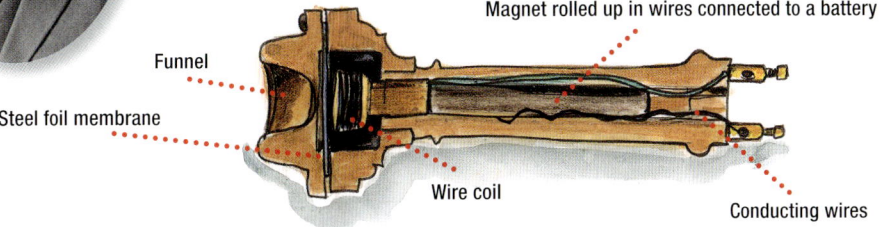

Steel foil membrane · Funnel · Magnet rolled up in wires connected to a battery · Wire coil · Conducting wires

In the telephone mouthpiece, the sound of the voice makes the air vibrate, and this causes a metal membrane to tremble. These vibrations are called 'sound waves'. The waves enter a funnel. When it vibrates, the metal membrane causes variations in the magnetic field of a magnet. The wire coil captures the vibrations, which produce varying electrical signals. The voice, converted into electrical signals, travels down the wire in the form of an electric current, and is reconverted into sound at the other end.

Experiment

Put your hand over your mouth and say 'hello'. Can you feel the vibrations from your voice on your hand? This is exactly what happens when a voice makes the membrane in the telephone mouthpiece vibrate.

Connect the telephones to the correct date.

Bell's telephone, 1876 • Crank telephone, 1890 • Candlestick telephone, 1905

Screen telephone, 1920 • Plastic telephone, 1930 • Cordless telephone, 1985 • Mobile phone, 1995

27

SATELLITES

Celestial bodies in orbit are natural satellites. Under the effect of gravity, the planets revolve around another planet with a greater mass. The Moon is a satellite of the Earth. It revolves around the Earth.
Telecommunication satellites act as relays for telephones and television. They receive radio waves and send them to Earth. They are launched by rocket into space. Satellites orbit at 36,000 km above the equator, and always remain above the same spot on Earth.

The rocket needs to have an engine which can propel the satellite at a speed of around 40,250 km/h. This is the escape velocity it must reach to leave the atmosphere and enter space.

TIP
Beware! There are also spy satellites. They can listen to all phone conversations and read faxes. The army sometimes uses these to spy on other countries.

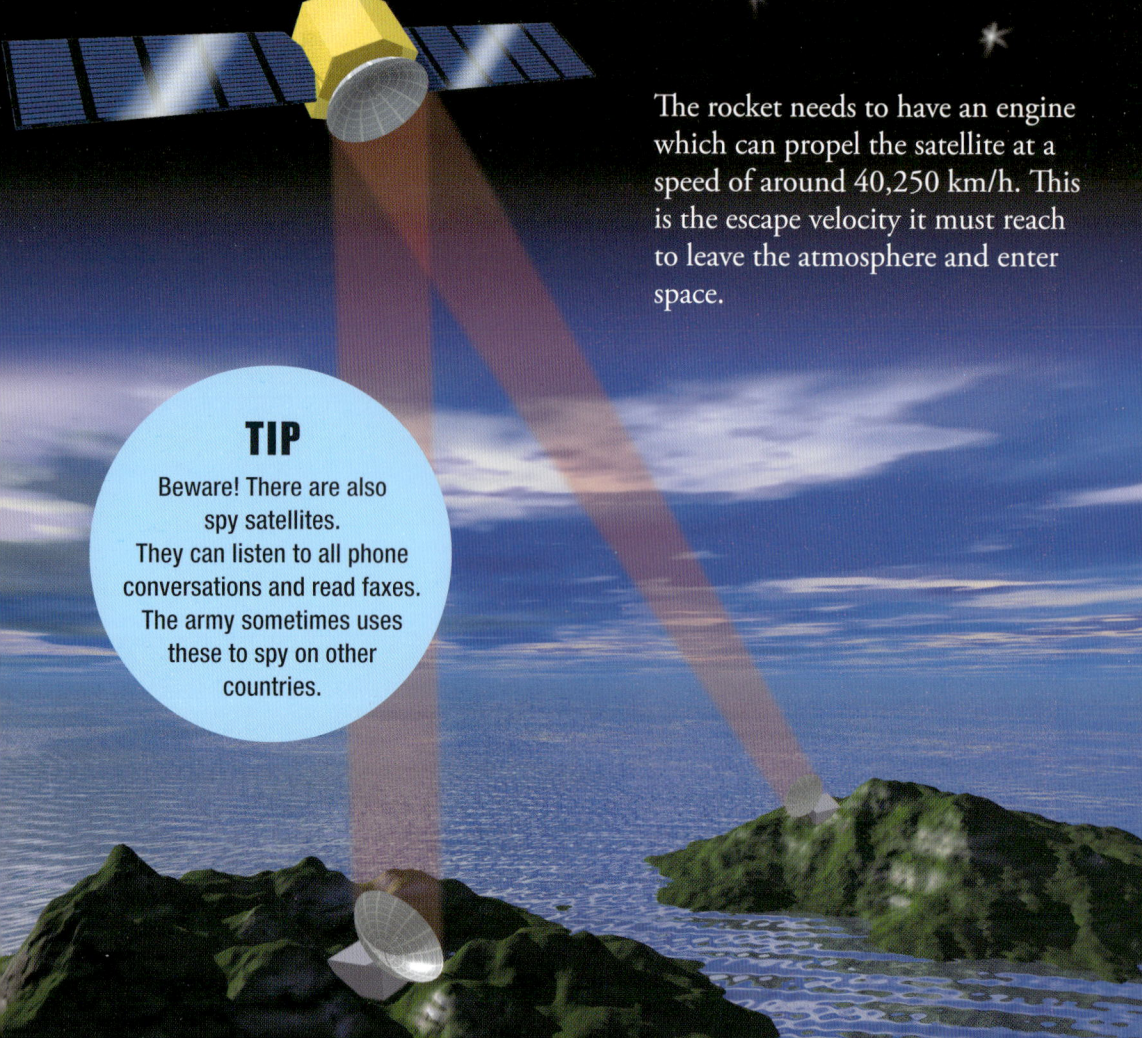

KINETICS – OPTICS

Imagine a rocket which will take you to the planets of your dreams.

THE BIG GAME

✏️ Draw a line between the inventors and their inventions, or what they studied.

Adrien de Gerlache

Charles Darwin

Galileo

Alessandro Volta

Zénobe Gramme

Samuel Morse

Joseph Plateau

The Montgolfier brothers

Cooke and Wheatstone

Alexander Graham Bell

Benjamin Franklin

Thomas Edison

OF INVENTIONS

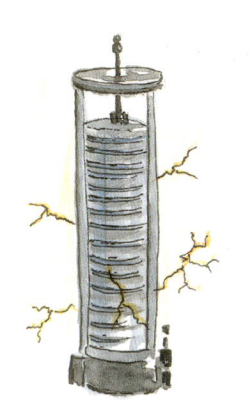

Texts: Catherine de Duve
Illustrations: Catherine de Duve
Proofreading: Sybille van Steenberghe
Coordination: Renaud Gahide, Sandra Lovato and Benoît Goffin

Photographic credits:
- p. 5: © Brussels, Royal Belgian Institute of Natural Sciences. L. Becker, reconstruction of the first Bernissart iguanodon skeleton, Nassau Chapel, Brussels, 1884.
- p. 6: Portrait of Charles Darwin.
- p. 10: © Brussels, Royal Observatory of Belgium. Small portable transit telescope by Toughton and Simms, commissioned by Quetelet in 1837.
- p. 11: © European Space Agency. The sun.
- p. 12: Portrait of Joseph Plateau.
- p. 12: © Ghent, Museum for the History of Sciences. Phenakistoscope discs.
- p. 14: © Brussels, Archives of the Royal Palace. Photograph of Professor Auguste Piccard. Phenakistoscope discs.
- p. 16: © Collection of Baron Gaston de Gerlache de Gomery. Portrait of Adrien de Gerlache de Gomery at Chriostana (Oslo)
- p. 17: The Belgica overwintering in Antarctica. 1898-1899.
- p. 19: Portrait of Alessandro Volta.
- p. 19: Photograph, portrait of Thomas Edison.
- p. 20: Portrait of Zénobe Gramme.
- p. 24: © Brussels, Albert 1st Royal Library. L. Melsen, lightning conductor on the belfry of Brussels Town Hall, 1877.
- p. 26: Portrait of William Cooke.
- p. 26: Portrait of Charles Wheatstone.
- p. 26: Portrait of Samuel Morse.
- p. 27: Portrait of Alexander Graham Bell.

With thanks to:
Robert Halleux, Philippe Tomsin, Jan Vandersmissen, Geneviève Lacroix, Mélanie Berghmans, Julie Dufour, Camille Degueldre and Véronique Lux for their invaluable collaboration in producing this book.